City
Bristol today in poems and pictures

An anthology of new poems by Bristol poets

Selected and edited by
Peter Hunter and David Johnson
Photographs by
Ralph Colmar, Sally Mundy, Dory English, Peter Hunter

PARALALIA
supported by
Creative Bristol, Arts & Business,
Amcor Flexibles Europe, Bart Spices, Ocean Estate Agents.

First published in 2004 by Paralalia, 1 Elgin Park, Bristol BS6 6RU

Doreen Baidoo   Rachel Bentham   Rosemary Dun   Mac Dunlop   Helen Dunmore   Lucy English
Helen Gregory   Philip Gross   Alyson Hallett   Fiona Hamilton   Rupert Hopkins   Ralph Hoyte
Peter Hunter   David C. Johnson   Tony Lewis-Jones   Bertel Martin   Annie McGann   Tom Phillips
Christine E. Ramsey-Wade   Ian Sills   Joe Solomon   Alan Summers   John Terry
Mark Warner   Claire Williamson

Ralph Colmar   Sally Mundy   Dory English   Peter Hunter

ISBN 0-9548117-0-4
British Library Cataloguing in Publication Date
A catalogue record for this book is available from the British Library

Designed by Peter Hunter and David C. Johnson
Cover Design by Peter Hunter
Front cover photo: Montpelier from Kingsdown - Ralph Colmar
Back cover photo: The Groves, Hartcliffe - Peter Hunter
Printed by Butler & Tanner Limited, Frome, Somerset

Forward

Ever since I first encountered Bristol in 1991 I have found it the most poetic of cities. Why is this? The simple fact is that beautiful places inspire artists. It's little wonder that the Romantic Movement was founded in the city with the publication of Lyrical Ballads, containing Coleridge's 'Rime of the Ancient Mariner' and Wordsworth's first great poem 'Tintern Abbey'. Both Coleridge and Wordsworth chose to live in Bristol's Georgian splendour; Chatterton, the 'marvellous boy', and Southey were born in the city. Southey, later poet laureate, declared that: 'I know of no mercantile place so literary…no city in England is to be compared with Bristol for singularity and beauty…no one ever more dearly loved his native place than I do'.

Nowadays we have a successful poetry festival and Bristol musicians lead the world in songwriting.

Not all poets have loved the city. Chatterton was disenchanted enough to leave Bristol. Richard Savage, poverty stricken and depressed about Bristol, claimed it was a city of:

'Upstarts and mushrooms, proud relentless hearts,
Thou blank of Sciences, thou dearth of Arts!'

But most love the place. Poetry was a strong part of the city's European Capital of Culture bid. We were amazed at the quality and extent of the work that we found - as were the judges. Fed up with the usual executive summary given in such documents, we asked local poet Fiona Hamilton - two of her works are in this book - to write a poem instead. Fiona's words showed just why Bristol should have been shortlisted; and we were.

Poetry occupies an important part of the delivery of Bristol's 2008 promise. We want to get more people reading and writing. Our annual Great Reading Adventure encourages everyone to read the same book. And our 2005 programme celebrating creativity in the city will have a celebration of words in all forms.

There's another reason why Bristol is a poetic city. There's a spirit of collaboration and debate, of performance and group reading, and of publishing in this wonderful city. Many of these poems have come out of the Poetry Slam tradition - those raucous, loud, sometimes verbally violent evenings, that are never less than fun and excellent and . . . well, poetic.

Here is a range of poems that express the Bristol of people's dreams, lives, troubles, fears and visions.
All of them represent Bristol poetry at its best. All of them inspired by a city that is a natural home for reading and writing.

Andrew Kelly *Creative Bristol*

"Poetry has the potential to reach out to people in a unique way. Bristol is fortunate in having so many contemporary poets and writers. This book will give some of them a much wider audience and at the same time encourage sponsorship of the arts by the business community."
Edward Shaw
Chairman, Bart Spices

"Amcor Flexibles has had a major manufacturing plant in Bristol for many years. We are delighted to be able to support this book, which we believe demonstrates yet another side of the creative resources of this city."
John Durston
Deputy Chief Executive, Amcor Flexibles Europe

Amcor Flexibles Europe Ltd, Bart Spices Ltd and Paralalia have received an investment from Arts & Business New Partners to further develop their creative partnership. Arts & Business New Partners is funded by Arts Council England and the Department for Culture, Media and Sport.

Ocean Estate Agents and Paralalia have received an investment from Arts & Business to further develop their creative partnership.

Arts & Business is the world's most successful and widespread creative network. They help business people support the arts and the arts inspire business people, because good business and great art together create a richer society.

Introduction

This book has its origins in Bristol's bid to be European City of Culture 2008 and the editors' involvement in organising a City of Culture Slam in 2002. That performance poetry competition, which pitted teams of poets from ten of the other competing cities in England, Wales and Northern Ireland against a Bristol team, made us realise how much there was to celebrate about our home town and how poetry could be used to create a vibrant word picture of the city.

We were aware of the depth and breadth of poetic talent in Bristol through our active involvement in the poetry scene, but the full extent of Bristol's bardic pool is, like Coleridge's caverns, immeasurable to man. Which was a problem when it came to inviting poets to contribute to **City: *Bristol today in poems and pictures.***
How could we choose from this host of poets? In the end, we went for a mix of the nationally celebrated, the locally renowned and a small number of new writers. We consoled ourselves with the thought that when this first Paralalia book was a sell-out success, we could then produce another with a different selection of great Bristol poets!

Having chosen which poets to invite to contribute, we then had to think about who to ask to provide us with great photographic images of Bristol today. We wanted pictures that spoke to the poems and we wanted images that would spark the poets. We also wanted the pictures to show us a wide spread of areas, people and activities in Bristol today, without ignoring all of the most iconic aspects of the cityscape. In the end, we were fortunate to involve two very different photographers, Sally Mundy and Ralph Colmar, in the project from the start and to have the input from Dory English, a young photographer at Filton College. In addition, it was impossible to stop co-editor, Peter Hunter from snapping at the photographic heels of Bristol. We think that the end results of all their work has given to the world an excellent and unusual view of the city.

We developed a very logical plan for the book. We would have pictures of Bristol through the seasons; cultural activities; at work; at play. We would have Bristol people at work and at play. We would cover all the geography of Bristol…and then we realised that we only had space for 40 photos and 40 poems. And later on we started to remember what it was like to work with poets! Most of whom are lovely, interesting genii of the word, but who cannot be told. As we found out, ask a poet to write about people in Stockwood, they'll come up with a brilliant verse about dustbins in Dundry. Ask a poet to be positive and celebratory through and through and she or he will recall in iambic pentameter a nightmare ride on a 93 bus to the end of the earth. But in the end, two years after the initial spark of an idea, we believe we have achieved an anthology of new verse with pictures of Bristol today that can make us proud of the city and at the same time not blind to some of its imperfections.

Paralalia could never have succeeded with this publishing enterprise without the consistent encouragement and funding support from the outset of Andrew Kelly and the Bristol Cultural Development Partnership.
Raising the funds that has enabled this book to be published was a long process but we were delighted that three Bristol-based business, Bart Spices, Amcor Flexibles and Ocean Estate Agents, have backed us and shown their support for poetry and the arts in Bristol. In addition, we were most fortunate that Arts & Business were prepared to invest in the project with matching funding through their New Partners and Strike a Match schemes. We would like to thank them all.

PARALALIA is a poetry partnership formed by Bristol poets, Peter Hunter and David Johnson to promote and encourage live poetry performance and to bring poetry to the public ear and eye in new and unusual ways.

David Johnson is a performance poet, writer, singer/song-writer and international business consultant. He lives in Bristol with his wife, children and collection of brightly coloured shirts. He is a co-founder of Paralalia, the originator of the City of Culture Slam, and a trustee of Streets Alive, bringing arts to the streets of Bristol.

David has appeared as a featured artist at Bristol Poetry Festival, Cheltenham Festival of Literature, Bath Fringe Festival, Kingston Arts Festival, London, Swindon Literature Festival and Ashton Court Community Festival. He has featured at Nuyorican Poetry Café, New York
He is a poetry slam multi winner (including Oxford All Stars Champion 2004), poetry co-ordinator of Streets Alive, Bristol, and is currently co-writing a play for broadcast in October 2004 on BBC Radio 4.
He has published 3 collections of poetry and a CD of songs co-written with musical partner Michael Godwin.

Peter Hunter is a performance poet and ceramicist/artist. He works in a studio in Central Bristol, and writes in his bedroom.
He is a founder member of Paralalia, and has been involved in running several national and international poetry events.

Peter has appeared as a featured artist at Glastonbury Festival, Bristol Poetry Festival, Cheltenham Festival of Literature, Leicester Comedy Festival, Bath Literature Festival, Bath Fringe Festival and Ashton Court Community Festival.
He has also appeared as a guest poet at Munich's 'Literaturehaus' and 'Speakandspin', Regensburg's 'Superslam', Prague's Club Zelezna, Pure Poetry, London, as a guest of Academi, Cardiff, Bristol Can Openers, Greenwich Park anti-GMO rally and Easton Community Festival.

He is a poetry slam multi-winner, including the title UK All-comers Slam Champ 2002/3, co-organiser of The New Jazz Slams, Bristol, was a writer and performer in The Phat-Lip Floor Show, Bristol, and is currently co-writing a play for broadcast on BBC Radio 4.

Contents

City
Bristol today in poems and pictures

An anthology of new poems by Bristol poets

Cover Up *

I come from the East,
a subcutaneous river
of hidden tongues

running beneath the city.
I could have been a
blue line, a blue line,

back bared to the sun,
brick of bridge,
my rain-swelled body

pushing against ridged
banks. I could have held
your face, the moon -

could have washed
truth into the bright
light of day.

Alyson Hallett

*Prior to the millenium, Bristol City Council decided not to open up the river Frome which runs beneath the city centre and instead opted to
install shallow ponds and low-flying fountains.

photo Sally Mundy

Bristol Docklands

Pero's Bridge -
the dock's ice gathers in
new year resolutions

attic window -
a winter ledge pigeon
overlooks the city

falling down
onto rush hour traffic
seagull feathers

waterbus ferries-
someone at the tiller
nods at John Cabot

summer rain -
the muted siren of a fire engine
over Bristol Bridge

cappuccino -
kids' feet splashing
by a jetty

city of bridges -
three four five swallows
spread out

February night
wind chimes and tackle echo
across the dock

sunlight breaks
on a bird
and its portion of the roof

the shortsighted man
points out a heron to me
some distance away

bright breeze
a sighted person fingers
the statue's eyes

floating harbour
a sunfall's last glints over
wind dimpled water

autumn twilight ...
swan shapes separate
for the lone boatman

Alan Summers

photo Sally Mundy

Centripetal force

Studying geography in a small-town school,
cities obeyed logical propositions.
Kristaller's Central Place Theory, for instance,
had them as hubs towards which
dutiful populations tended
for no better reason than that they
simply existed. Real cities refuse
to behave. They sprawl outwards,
ensnaring satellite towns,
hide behind ring roads,
let their hinterlands down
with boarded-up factories
and too few hospitals.
We've given up trying to control them.
We prefer to let them run amok,
spinning like galaxies around
concreted squares, the rumble
and flip of skateboards,
traffic jams, commuters, call centres,
one-sided babble into hands-free sets,
rebranded agencies and institutions,
anxious lovers in poor disguises,
bus stops, billboards, council buildings,
credit card facilities and cash points;
and somewhere, at the nub,
above suited workers and heads-down shoppers,
the telling silence,
the silence of a forever-stopped clock.

Tom Phillips

photo Sally Mundy

A La Carte with Baudelaire
(Dejeuner a Quartier Vert)

The soup was Crème de Trompette de la Mort,
with black bread and sparkling Evian,
followed by rare flesh, woodland creature,
with fungi, green strain of Stilton.
We savoured the raw nerve of shellfish,
held on the tongue in a wince of jus.
Then nuts and berries - roots and tubers.
Entrée of roe and the sinew of amphibia,
with julienne of nettle, bruised belladonna,
nasturtium, camomile, mint and feverfew.
Copper through cheese - wire and cream.
Steel blade - knife - muscle and blood.
He said 'We are what we eat - you see?'
I said, 'I know. I'll eat you. You eat me.'

Annie McGann

photo Sally Mundy

Steff

You makes I laff,
you makes I cry.
My life ain't much,
but it ain't nothing, if you ain't in it.

You makes I smile,
you makes I frown.
We bin together for years,
an' I still enjoys meself with you.

You makes I love,
you makes I hate.
You're all I ever wanted,
all I'll ever need.
You makes I feel alright.

Bertel Martin

Royate Hill

Today, you cross the gate, instead
of keeping on up the street, and walk
the gravel path on the bridge, through
the blackberry brambles and buddleia, to watch
the sun as it glares at the trademarks of life -
allotments, roof tiles, gravestones, magpies,
dragged clouds, rude graffiti.

The city looks like distant mountains,
with hills of green behind. Instead
of sea, the roar of tyres and motors
combine with seagulls, audible only
when the winds and all their talk
of rain defer to warming sunshine.
Nothing new here - just

a nature walk in town. No different
from the rest, except this mix
of care and concrete, and the damp.
Except today, you took a right,
you made this walk for the first time -
nothing but your choice remains
between this home and strangeness.

Christine E. Ramsey-Wade

5am Bristol

Standing on Brandon Hill
watching the city
blush into morning

wishing everything
was the same, but different.

Security isn't to be found
in other people.
It's the way the soul connects
to 5am, Bristol.

Peacock backdrop to the harbour;
familiar lights far away on Dundry;
Constitution Hill flying vertical.

Sitting barefoot on the grass
cradling a memory in my lap
lovers recumbent
demerara faces to the sun
unaware of ageing
or being anything but lovers.

5am Bristol
the moon is cut-out
an inverse Matisse.

The birds are winching
the day in
with their singing

Clocks across the city
are whispering
5am Bristol.

Claire Williamson

photo Sally Mundy

Cranes of Bristol
If you fold a thousand paper cranes your wishes will come true

The cranes have come to Bristol
Migrating from construction sites far and near
Red, white, green, yellow, blue they stand
Long beaks extended, quivering in the breeze
Like Trumpeter, Whooping and Dancing cranes,
Birds of legend and mystery
Bringers of fertility, fidelity and longevity,
Carriers on their backs of heroes to the heavens
The Siberian crane flies a thousand miles, up to three miles high
And crosses the tallest mountains to build its nests of twigs and grass
The Bristol crane constructs dream homes of steel, stone and glass
And then trundles off at 15 miles per hour along the ground

The cranes have come to Bristol
Bringers of good fortune and a better life?

David Johnson

photo Ralph Colmar

Inner City Bristol

Inner city Bristol
Diamond of the basin
Refractions reflections
Refractions reflecting
The diversity
Of the inner city
The colours
Of the community
Where else
But the inner city
Can you buy pizza
Topped with cataloo
Or ackee and saltfish
With the shop next door
Selling saris
And the place next to that
Playing reggae music
All stapled together
In Stapleton Road

Inner city Bristol
Diamond at the bottom of the Basin
First to be seen
Last to be considered
Misunderstood
Overlooked
Mislaid
Driven through
Skirted around
And
Misrepresented

Doreen Baidoo

photo Peter Hunter

City

the person sitting next to you
may be fluent in a language
you are unfamiliar with

a city is a place of continual motion
where things form and disperse
connecting and separating

the language you speak
may not be the one I understand best

the external city
is a place of
buildings roads
signs bridges
rivers traffic
people

the internal city
is the one you build in your head
out of imagination
and desire
subject to no planner's control

the city is an opportunity
for millions of chance collisions

Brig - stow
bridge place
some collisions
produce sparks

the person sitting next to you
may be fluent in a language
you are unfamiliar with
listen
look
open
love
and see

Fiona Hamilton

photo Sally Mundy

City Lilacs

In crack-haunted alleys, overhangs,
plots of sour earth that pass for gardens,
in the space between wall and wheelie bin,

where men with mobiles make urgent conversation,
where bare-legged girls shiver in April winds,
where a new mother stands on her doorstep and blinks
at the brightness of morning, so suddenly born -

in all these places the city lilacs are pushing
their cones of blossom into the spring
to be taken by the warm wind.

Lilac, like love, makes no distinction.
It will open for anyone.
Even before love knows that it is love
lilac knows it must blossom.

In crack-haunted alleys, in overhangs,
in somebody's front garden
abandoned to crisp packets and cans,

on landscaped motorway roundabouts,
in the depth of parks
where men and women are lost in transactions
of flesh and cash, where mobiles ring

and the deal is done: here the city lilacs
release their sweet, wild perfume
then bow down, heavy with rain.

Helen Dunmore

photo Dory English

St. Werburgh's Climbing Centre

I clip the rope to my belt
You thread it through yours.

You are starting to climb,
Your hands searching,
Your toes nuzzling.

I pull the rope in bit by bit
Knowing if you slip you are safe,
My weight will hold yours.

You are confident.
You do not look down.
You are nearing the top.

One day I will have let the rope right out
And you will be climbing solo.

Fiona Hamilton

photo Sally Mundy

Gloucester Road Beggars

1: Mixed Reactions

There are poor folk who are busking
poor folk who are juggling,
but mostly they are begging
outside shops on Gloucester Road.

There are people who are giving,
some crouch beside them, talking,
but mostly they are passing
as they shop on Gloucester Road.

Some think about them, caring.
Some think about them, blaming.
But it's mostly mental shrugging
when they think of Gloucester Road.

Charities acting locally,
the 'czar' who's acting nationally
bring no piece of the action
for most on Gloucester Road.

2: Mixed Feelings

When a beggar sits in the wind and rain
and something inside me feels the pain,
I give.

When this beggar sits in the wind and rain
and I think he's using the weather for gain,
I pass.

When a beggar asks "Can you spare a fag?"
and I think how I feel without a drag
I give.

When this beggar asks "Can you spare a fag?"
and I feel it as a wearisome nag,
I pass.

When I'm begged the price of a cup of tea
and I think but for luck this could have been me,
give? pass?

Joe Solomon

photo Ralph Colmar

Winging It

Damselflies are into sex. Whoever said
only birds can fornicate and fly
never watched electric-blue pointers
lock together, stiff with desire,

flicking in from dimensions outside
our own. Their polished compass needles
point at reeds, slip through folded
space; repeat from another angle

a shimmering two-fingered salute
to ideas of decency. A jump-jet
display of aerobatic orgasm
hot enough to make her tail curl.

An inch above the pond, high
on the wild anti-gravity of sex
her tail's tip pierces water -
and a thousand eggs scramble.

John Terry

photo Ralph Colmar

Sea Walls

Late summer. And we shall go to Sea Walls
Down the avenue of chestnut trees
Where the leaves are turning yellow
And have already begun to fall.

And we shall sit on the bench by the ice cream van.
Sea Walls. The sea will never rise as high as here.
The cliff face. The high rock.
The edge of the city garden playground.
We shall let our thoughts hang
Like the climbers on the red ropes.
Poised for a moment looking down
At the muddy river flowing towards the cranes of Avonmouth.
And in the distance the silver sunlight on the Severn.
And the clouds on the high black hills in Wales.

I was eighteen once. Beautiful and proud.
My first summer in an empty town.
In my old jeans, a lacy shirt and a hat with a flower,
I strolled every day across the downs.
Smiling like it was my own garden.

Three little white haired boys
Playing with a kite.
It won't go up! It won't go up! And then it does.
They stand and watch it soar.
Three faces wide with wonder
At the shape of red hanging in the blue.

photo Sally Mundy

I loved you once.
We loved each other with a passion that was quiet and real.
We tumbled out of bed in your Redland flat
And somehow made it across the downs
For breakfast in the Primrose café.
We sat there. Silent. Bombed out on sex.
And love and love and love.
You had it so bad you could barely eat
Your scrambled eggs.

Come with me now to Sea Walls
Down the avenue of chestnut trees
Where the leaves are turning yellow
And have already begun to fall.

Where the young men play football
And the young girls stroll heads held high.
They have never tasted sorrow.
Where the lovers are making promises they cannot keep.
Where the little children run with kites
And their parents will remember
Far beyond tomorrow.

Lucy English

photo Peter Hunter

The Bristolian Job

It's a long story, how I got here,
All twists and turns,
Odd accents,
Hair-raising stunts
And luck
(Most of it bad).

I'm not sure when I arrived,
Drawn by the siren songs of Portbury,
Lured inland by the scent of the city,
But I know
My friends will join me
In time.
I am not lost.

I am in the city.
I prefer cities.
I was built for the metropolis;
Skipping through needle-eye gaps,
Nipping round tight corners,
The aggrieved hooting of the cumbersome
Music to my ears

Now I feel alone,
Missing my other two-thirds.
Watching for their triumphant return,
Waiting
For the last-reel happy ending.
Waiting.

(I am not lost.)

Ian Sills

photo Peter Hunter

Lockleaze Resolution

Wilf and his dog walk by,
taking part of the day with them up the road.
On the green behind the houses,
spirits wander
between the aging oaks and ash trees
growing wild,
in the once manicured landscape.

The motorway cuts through it like a rip saw.
forming vapours of tin sealed breath
exhaled into the sky.

It's busy at this time of day.
The air carrying a non-stop rumble over the crest of the downs.
Up on our road, cars park like dotted lines outside the zig zags by the school gate.
Parents and children taught to start the day clogging the street.

A bus passes up to the Square.
Passing all the new year rubbish bins
filled with resolutions and promise.
Passing all the garden sheds
where green moss rides up the brickwork.
Passing all the tarmac-ed scars
of telephone lines, cable nets, waterworks, and gas pipes

Charting, beneath each step
the underground history
of our changing landscape.

Mac Dunlop

photo Sally Mundy

Thirty-Seven Year Old Play Worker Shirks His Responsibilities in Victoria Park

Mickey's found a page from a porn mag stuffed
in a bush and the boys are passing it around,

Asa's freewheeling down the hill
on a rusty bicycle without any tyres,

Dale's in a shopping trolley
and one of the girls is crying,

and I'm in goal on the concrete court
and nothing's getting past me.

Mark Warner

Animal Fan Mail

It was audition day at Bristol Zoo
And every star struck creature
Was determined to secure a role
In Wallace and Gromit's new feature.
The penguins were dressed up as chickens.
The sheep had hitched down from the farm.
The snakes got all rattled.
The peregrines prattled
And the sloth raised a paw in alarm.
The chimps scratched their heads in bemusement,
At the animals practising lines,
While the zookeepers polished their wellies
And finished de-rusting the signs.
The spiders were skittery.
Hippos were jittery.
All were set out to impress.
The butterflies fluttered.
The woodpeckers stuttered.
The fish twitched their fins in distress.
The flamingos were practising synchronised strokes.
The hyenas were psyching them out,
And the shiniest goldfish in Bristol
Was perfecting her prettiest pout.
The lioness whined and sheep bleated,
Til the seals got all shy and retreated,
But the camera crew soon had them jumping through hoops
Using sardines that they had secreted.
The next day when they opened the cast was selected,
The microphones gone
And the signs re-erected.
The visitors came and contemplated,
Cogitated, ruminated,
For never before had they seen a zoo
With animals so animated.

Helen Gregory

photo Sally Mundy

A Chance of Dragons *Station Road, Chinese New Year*

The dragon stamps, it stamps and flares
in a cul-de-sac backstreet - the viaduct walls

in smokestone, falls of ivy, a place with an air
of being cobbled though it's not, somewhere

a van could park until its tyres go down,
between the faces beaming from their billboard

on the corner five times our size, five times sleeker
like gods of good fortune, and the winos' secret

trash-and-mattress cave; outside a square and low
white warehouse, on a ramp of forklift pallets, there

the year begins; it comes out bright and papery
as painted fire, a dragon that could fold into a largish

suitcase in a cargo hold; here it comes, out of sour-
sweet-and-musty emporium smells, a world

that opens inwards implausibly far, to candies,
movie mags and cleavers, diligence and abalone shells,

dried duck with beak and feet on but flattened
with a tarry look like roadkill, cut price flights

to Hong Kong (two way), lanterns, sacks
of bean sprouts big as bolsters, and a shrine;

here it comes, with half a man still visible
inside, part swallowed, half of him its legs that stamp

out the swagger and ripple and sway, for us all,
the idlest passers-by, the most hurrying-home

wherever home may be, however far;
and now the train wheels spark and thump

on the viaduct: firecrackers, promising
the chance of dragons, anywhere.

Philip Gross

photo Ralph Colmar

Subculturecity

High pressure sky; baby wool blue.
　　　Wintry sunshine beckons the
　　　leisured to join the beggars
　　　outside.

Pavement café: luxury. A tall steel
　　　mushroom bestows warmth on
　　　the old gent in a fur hat, ramrod
　　　straight.

Luvvie boys, next table, sounds like:
　　　Restoration; script highlighted
　　　in lime, fags and pretty
　　　stubble.

Far fetched tomato and coconut soup,
　　　baguette elastic as sin; organic,
　　　satisfies the urge to bite,
　　　hard.

Kindly pink dusts the housetops, as day sags
　　　between blocks. A black woman; chic,
　　　purposeful, strides towards Blackboy
　　　Hill.

The city sits lipserviced on that trade, the
　　　BBC lounging along Whiteladies
　　　Road, the taxpayers' bedtime
　　　story.

photo Ralph Colmar

After workers slump into theme pubs
    happy pint hanging over their
    waistbands weary as wedding
    rings.

Home to St Somewhere, shoeboxed near
    the dull park dappled with skaters
    baggy as doggydoo,
    spliffin.

Rage up the motorway to Yate and Bradley
    Stoke, sadly broke cul de sac white
    ghetto shopping on the cream
    sofa.

Dripping dark tunnels ripple with graffiti -
    monsters robocops and words
    oversprayed before we catch
    on.

All over town, the underworld wakes up, rolls up,
    gets out - skanking what stuff? Your
    stuff - mugging's just a tax,
    man.

Municipal beds are bottled, shit bins melted,
    but kids still flower in the park;
    blossoms gathering to scent the city
    throb.

Coatless townies with bare legs screech
    into poppy lip gloss seventies retro
    cheese big booted pill long
    dancefloors.

Later still studded pink paddles smack naughty
    big boys at Spank's leather S&M
    rubber Religion schoolgirl babyoil
    clubnight.

Taxis rank while pissy fountains check their pelvic
    floors - and hold - orderly as urinals in
    the totalitarian style centre waiting for
    night/life.

Loving it up, dancing 'til dawn litters the streets;
    urban warriors gathering; beats meet
    sweat meet soul: mindbodyspirit -
    the new mix.

Rachel Bentham

photo Ralph Colmar

That Avon Gorge Poem

Mornin', Gorgeous!

Ralph Hoyte

photo Peter Hunter

Redwings

Outside my window
a flock of angels
feasting on the pyracantha's
red berries.

Old devil blackbird,
whose territory this is,
frozen
on the garage roof,
in shock
or helpless rage -
longing for a shotgun
(who can tell?)

A warmth of feathers
colouring icy air:
Brown shading into brown -
brown set against cream;
sudden blush of red ochre.
And throat to tail
brush-speckled
water colour
on hand-made paper.

Angels,
dining on the pyracantha.

Only the blackbird
rejoiced
when they left -
sharp accountant's eye
on the remaining berries.

His evening song
longer
than usual.

John Terry

photo Sally Mundy

Hartcliffe

The fields behind Hartcliffe
Are as green as fields anywhere
The tree-lined streets are as wide as any Clifton Avenue
The Bastard Service tree by the Gatehouse is as perfect as any in Eden
The sky is as blue and the view is as wide from the top of a block in Hartcliffe as anywhere
The people are as warm, the families as close and their feelings as deep and intense as anywhere
Want a friend, want a job, want true love, want some fame: hopes as fantastic and mundane as anywhere
Hartcliffe has dreams as sweet and as sour as anywhere ....BUT HARTCLIFFE IS NOT ANYWHERE.

David Johnson

photo Sally Mundy

Happy Anniversary

Kuumba
Thirty years
The Pearl
The pearl anniversary
Black Pearl
A rarity
A piece of grit
From the Rasta's grit
Their frustration
Produced this
This pearl
This Black Pearl
In the heart of Bristol
A rarity
In the whole
Of the West Country
Kuumba
Creativity
A Pearl
A Black Pearl

Doreen Baidoo

photo Ralph Colmar

Medusa goes to the hairdressers.
for all at Altered Image, Alma Vale Road.

Tired of her dread locks and permanently stoned friends she booked
an appointment in the salon made ready with curlers and tongs.
Oh… Here she comes…Unruly mop tamed by a scarf wrapped
turban style. C'est chic! She wore shades and so did we; blindfolded
with cucumber eye masks our ladies lulled by the drone of dryers.
Gingerly, Vince teased her writhing barnet with a cleft stick. Having
watched nature shows on the BBC he knew to hold each snake curl
behind the eyes. Using Indian music to hypnotic effect, her locks
were lopped and, one by one, slithered slyly across the floor;
swept straight up by Mrs C and put in a bin bag by the door.
Her crop looked like the underside of a bathmat; strange nubs
of amputation healing quickly, each stump a button mushroom bump
as her hairdo hissed deep within the sack. Darrell said when it grew
back, perhaps she'd like to have a bee hive, something like that?

Annie McGann

photo Sally Mundy

Ode to a Jay Off Grosvenor Road

Punk-blue paraffin pink jay
Nests in the woody green off Grosvenor Road.
Listens to the city sounds and
Jerk chicken and salt fish and charcoal smells
Of Carnival. Dances on roots rock-steady
Wing flight to the sweeping sand rhythms of drum and bass
And hip-hop culture. Swoops over competing clash of
Merry making, purple smooth lipstick, silver sequinned,
Black, gold and green dust sound system crew.

Her chicks laid back in manger nest,
No room for the blues,
Groove to dove-tailed rooted trip hop
City slick street beats,
Enjoy ska sunstroke rain drizzle heat,
Grow natty dreads,
Deck out,
Check out in amber braided
Dread lock dead lock extensions
And mean ugly Rayban cool ice sunglasses.
Party at Ajax's alleyway Blues
Till Red Stripe dawn mingles with the rising sun

Sip with open beak
Left over
Moss stained wooden bench
Outside Star and Garter Guinness
Leave that emerald isle
Rural idyll behind.

Rupert Hopkins

photo Ralph Colmar

Evening Light

When days are still, there is a clear and tender evening light
That polishes the beauty in each subtle shade and tone.
That flatters buildings; pulling them up to their fullest height
Plumping up the red in brick and burnishing the gold in stone.

This light insinuates, idealising every city view
It sharpens edges; flattens homes to folded-paper thin.
Deftly drawn in glowing ink on waning parchment blue
Terraces become tattoos on soft perspective's skin.

In gardens, swarms commemorate this subtle light in dance
Diamond flecks that spin and swirl in absence of a breeze;
Blackbirds, filled with praise, rejoice in liquid luminescence,
Tall in silhouetted jet on backlit emerald trees.

Kerbside weeds, heroic with long shadows, feel it pass.
It soothes the tips of grass and kisses closing daisies' eyes
Releasing them with kindness from the day's demanding task,
Reminding us it's time to rest with silent lullabies.

Traffic whispers reverentially, respectful of the calm.
The moon, a phantom sickle, charms the night across the sky.
A single wren 'chip-chip's and then retrieves its brief alarm
As the palest pricks of stars respond to daylight's parting sigh.

Peter Hunter

photo Peter Hunter

Dunhelmus Bristoliensuis

Young Tommy 'TomBoy' Chatterton slithers into the 252 BHP metallic
lapis blue 5 speed Tiptronic Porsche Boxster S he's 'borrowed' from
Dick Lovett Specialist Cars just behind his dad's falling down house on
the Portwall and gi'es 'er some wellie EEEeeeowwww and he's doing
68 and hasn't even changed out of first yet what a burn up he's in
Knowle West on the playing field behind Airport Road before you can
say 'joyriders unite OK' shows off the full leather sports seats, 18" sport
design alloys and on-board computer to his mates Wordsworth,
Southey and Coleridge they get out the petrol can but this 40K second
hand job's too good to torch ye gettaload of that 360º handbrake turn
Wordsworth, Southey and Coleridge almost piss themselves in
admiration and Edward Orme gets just the right shade of black for
those twin smoking tracks on the tarmac in front of the well trashed
cinema on Filwood Broadway. Go, TomBoy, go - but make sure you
stay alive, or, at the very least, man, do a James Dean this time, not
just a shoot-up in some crappy dive in The Great Smog. "Now agayne
with bremie Force Severn in his auntient Course Rolls his rappyd
streeme alonge" indeed. Who did he think he was fooling?

Ralph Hoyte

photo Ralph Colmar

On Narrow Quay

Summer, and the Bristol harbourside
Is full of life and colour.
Although the weatherman has got it wrong again
And skies stay stubbornly overcast
There seems to be a mass determination
To enjoy ourselves. Looking at the crowds
Of eager faces by the market stalls
Money is plentiful, and the will to spend
Is unabated. Bristol is wealthy,
It has been so for centuries,
But what we purchase has modified somewhat
From the days these streets were thronged with trade
Of other kinds. The dockland thoroughfares,
Now bedecked with balloons and bunting,
Could tell some stories if the stones could speak.
The tired busker sings, 'Nothing ever changes'.
I drop a coin into his hat, walk on.

Tony Lewis-Jones

photo Sally Mundy

Nighttown

For all that it's dark,
the city's routine claustrophobia lifts
as you tack across Queen Square
to where the harbour's laced
with isobars of neon,
cash burning a hole in your pocket,
desire like one in your guts.

Still just off stage at the melodrama,
this feeling now is how - if asked -
you'd set about defining the possible:
all this before you, no such thing
as too much. The lure of the sirens'
dismal jazz, prospected chance
meetings, brief encounters,
beer, musk, tongues, hands, clichés:
the comfort of small hours small talk.
This is the threshold. From here,
the night embraces or swallows you whole.

Tom Phillips

photo Ralph Colmar

A Slice of Life

nine used durexes
on the wasteland
by the dead river
bring no metaphor to mind
just the smile
of my young neighbour
as we say polite hellos
on the
street

Bertel Martin

photo Peter Hunter

Southville

Lower Clifton
they said in the 80's
when estate agent speak ruled
OK
now it's Southville,
it's on the wrong side
of the river
not North, where it's trendy
to stay, or to buy
not as hip either
as high Totterdown
with its veggie cafes
and boho poets
Instead:
Southville's got East Street
where everything comes cheap
in a synthetic acrylic way
lacking the chic
of Gloucester Road bric-a-brac
or second hand retro shops
and organic grocers selling kumquats
a courgette's as exotic
as it gets
and yet
it's gert lush
of an evening
when you sits in the yard
an' you watch
air balloons puff
and sigh
Paaah!
orgasmic even
with chilled beer in hand
as they pass overhead, float on by
Pwawhh
Aaaaaaaaah.

Rosemary Dun

photo Ralph Colmar

Dance

this is serious business, this
matching mood and movement all
together, when the music calls

lines of light distract your eyes
entrancing flashes stop your thoughts
this is serious business, this

sound so deep it shakes your bones
your heart, your hair, your arms, the air
together, when the music calls

you stamp for all the wrongs, you clap
for all the joys you've ever seen
this is serious business, this

the dj smiles, connecting spells
the people shout, a building roar
together, when the music calls

and still it comes, and comes, and comes
a pause - and then all time is now
this is serious business, this
together, when the music calls

Christine E. Ramsey-Wade

photo Ralph Colmar

A Wash and Brush Up

Bristol brushes her teeth,
Washes her face,
Combs her hair,
Showers away her cares,
Prepares for another day.

Bristol paints her nails,
Shadows her eyes,
Applies lipstick to look her best
Under the light of a city night
In the south west.

Ian Sills

photo Peter Hunter

Neptune's Gert Big Ideawl*

Casunt thee swim slower en tha?
I be short o breath me babby.
Dress in this yur bikini see
Me bellees summat flabby.
Me lover I got asthmal bad.
Dunt thee get the pitcher?
The warters in me yer awl
An me yeerin int no richer.
Yur actin like a cyclepath,
Baint ye got no mercy.
Me froats dry yur blimmin spanner
Giss some glider I be firsty.
Plungin fru this warter
Mi'ed an puddies urt
Yur a quicken but its munt fur I
Swemmen in me skirt.

(*for translation see appendix xi)

Helen Gregory

photo Ralph Colmar

The Jewish Cemetery - The Dings

A tarnished ornament,
Hangs beside the ragged tin shack swordfish scrap yard,
Glistening in the last rays of this Indian Summer.

Concrete jungle memories
Adrift amongst the green moss headstones
Awash with past lives in far away places

From Russia, Poland and Nazi Occupied Europe
Carved in stone lost worlds
And forgotten dreams

While children climb fences
Looking for lost footballs
And chasing Joseph amazing dream coat butterflies.

Rupert Hopkins

photo Sally Mundy

Takeaway
(St Marks Rd.)

Daddy look, a dragon! Look a dragon, daddy, look!
Don't be silly son; it's just a picture in a book.

No daddy; look, a dragon! By that window, right up there!
Listen son, there's no such thing as dragons. Here or anywhere.

But daddy it's got claws and teeth; it's sort of green and red!
That's enough son. Pack it in. Did you hear what I said?

But daddy, I can see it; flying up above that shop!
Son, this isn't funny now. You're going to have to stop!

But dad, there really is a dragon. Look up there, you'll see.
Well, I'll be…, so there is. Now let's go in and get our tea.

Peter Hunter

Peter Hunter

Appendices

N.B. Index of Photographs. In an attempt to capture the mood of the poems, the photographers and editors have not always selected images of the areas of Bristol specifically mentioned in the poems.

Translation of 'Neptune's Gert Big Ideawl'

Neptune's Jolly Good Idea

Can you swim a touch more slowly?
I am rather breathless old chap.
Attired in this fetching bikini,
There is some excess flesh on one's lap.
I have terrible breathing difficulties.
I do hope you understand.
This water has entered my ear hole,
And there's no ear trumpet to hand.
You are rather harsh old fellow,
I am concerned what you may think,
But my throat is a little dry
Might I trouble you for a drink?
Hurrying through this water
Is like being hit by a rock
You are a speedy fellow but it's not easy
To swim in my frock

Helen Gregory

Poets Listed in Alphabetical order

Index of First Lines

Index of Photographs